Poems By The Fox: Songs From The Shadows

AF624653

Amanda Fisher

BookLeaf Publishing
India | USA | UK

Presentation by *BookLeaf Publishing*

Web: www.bookleafpub.com

E-mail: info@bookleafpub.com

ISBN: 9789363319721

First edition 2024

ACKNOWLEDGEMENT

I'd like to acknowledge two musicians from whom I have drawn in some of these poems.

The poem 'Subtract' includes lyrics from the song 'Breathe Me' by Sia. During my hardest days I played this song on repeat as it gave words to my pain.

The poem 'Up' draws on the song 'Here Comes The Sun' by the Beatles. I remember hearing this song at the end of 'Bee Movie' and it still chokes me up.

Thankyou, for your inspiration.

PREFACE

Trigger Warning

These poems deal with themes of mental illness and suicidality. If anything in this book causes you distress, please reach out and talk to someone you trust, or contact a helpline.
For a guide to what's available in your country go to www.findahelpline.com

Afloat

I don't want to do this anymore
This sentence runs over and over
In a brain both wild and blank

This time's not as bad as the last ones
She's not disappearing
But she's not engaging either

She wants to feel something, even pain
Anything to justify
The flat nothing filling her

Somehow this not-so-badness
Is harder than the horror
The incomprehensible pain

She's trying to drown
With a life jacket buoying her up
When all she wants is to sink

Crying In The Coffee Shop

I've been here before
So many times
Brushing away tears with my sleeve
Or else letting them fall
Hoping someone will see

I'm thinking about Harry Potter
His tears of grief
And all the pain he's seen and carried
And I'm wishing my tears were from the same thing
Instead of this

But I sit in this space
Staring out the window
At all the life bustling by
And feeling
Disconnected

An invisible barrier penning me in
I can no more grasp the life in front of me
Than reach my hand through the glass
And touch the people
Walking by

Emerging

It's like waking up
The first day of the holidays
Or Saturday morning
To the smell of freshly mown grass

That tingly feeling
A jolt in the belly
As days of freedom and sunlight
Stretch out ahead of you

I find myself talking to strangers
The atmosphere open and light
And a sense of possibility
Permeating every step

It seems too good to be true
Or else a pause in time
When reality is suspended
The interval in a concerto of chaos

So I jump in wholeheartedly
Swim around in it
Determined to soak up the ions
Until even my bones sing

Green

The mood chart
Tracked with colours
So often shades of sunset

It's a rarity
But it's here today
Sunshine in the colour of green

The morning air
Fresh and light
No doubt helped by clear skies

No different tactics
It's just time
Turning the colour up in my world

Hiding Place

You are my hiding place
A shelter from the storm
That rages on around me

But what of the storm
That threatens to drown
The storm flooding within

How do I remember
And hold onto truth
With a mind that tries to take me down

"Have faith" they say
"Choose truth" they declare
"Trust it will get better"

"Just give up" it says
"There's no point" it shrugs
"Choose death"

I want to believe it won't always be this way
The feelings will lift
And life return

But I'm running out of strength
Losing my grip
The yawning black abyss beckons

How To Halt Energy

How do you stop energy?
I need to know
To halt potential
At the place it would turn to motion

Electrical impulses firing and misfiring
Layers of chemical
I need a circuit breaker
Stop me in my tracks

I Bought A Diary

I bought a diary

A small thing, maybe
Trivial
A detail you might deem
Insignificant

But I share it

Because
So often lately
I have thought it unlikely
That I would need one

Not because I don't plan

I do
But because I couldn't imagine
Being here
Another year

So while it's small

Surface and shallow
This nine dollar bundle of paper

Is a decision
To stay

Labour Pains

She screams
Each wave gripping her every molecule
Until she can think of nothing else

The pain
So intense it overwhelms thought
Trying to breathe yet holding breath

Holding on
Curling, clenching, crying, numbing
Distracting from feelings she cannot bear

The sheet
Relaxation techniques to try
An insult to her agony

Real help
Is holding space within the unbearable
Let her scream and bear her through to relief

Last Vestiges (The Leaf)

It catches my eye
Vivid red and gold
And I stoop to pick it up
Only to see the colours seeping away into
crinkled brown

And I think of the dashboard in Riley's mind
In the movie "Inside Out"
How the lights fade in a wave
Until the last flicker is reignited by the touch of
sadness

Last vestiges
Of colour, life, and light
Speak determination
A dogged holding onto hope where it seems
pointless

For though brightness fades
And joy seems lost
There is hope in sadness
And in dying, the possibility of rebirth

Living For Lucy

Her sassy, golden curls
Reflect her sassy, golden heart

With angel face
Her gremlin moments
Only serve to make me love her more
- if that were possible

Appointed as her godmother -
Her 'fairy-godmuvver'
I took the honour
And embedded it in my heart

And with it I took the responsibility
- though I never would have called it that -
To love her, cherish her, guide her
And to show her how to do the same

But here today
In this place I know so horribly well
The place I hold in this golden, sassy life
Is saving mine

For what child could ever bear
The weight of such a choice
Carried out, though out of pain
By one both treasurer and treasured

Today,
I am living for Lucy

Moth

He lay there
In a puddle formed by heavy downpour
Wide wings with circles
Fluttering against my fingers
As I pick him up and place him in the garden

I've rescued him
I thought as my heart ached with sadness
For what might have been
Had I not found him
And he had come to an end

Yesterday again
I found him struggling in that same puddle
And I wondered
Had he been drawn to it
Or tried to escape and been pulled down

So I rescued him
Yet again placing him out of harm's way
And going on my way
Hoping that he would fly
And survive the dreadful storm

Today he was still
Wings outstretched, afloat in the water
And the grief came
I had tried to save him
But he had not been able to survive

Had he wanted to?
Or had the pull of the depths been too strong
His fragile wings
Beating so hard
But waterlogged losing strength

Until the fight died
Too much to survive and impossible to fly
A tiny life
Ending in struggle
The search for freedom and peace unsuccessful

Numb

I'd rather rain than dulling clouds
And tears than aching numb
The skies release their heavy load
Relief is easy won

Yet I am sitting underneath
A weight I cannot shake
So full and feeling fit to burst
Why can't my heart just break

As daylight fades and creeping chill
Starts biting at my skin
My spirit groans and longs to feel
The heat of hot tears' sting

Oh heavy heart so burdened with
A sadness thick and deep
Have mercy, please, and let me be
Unravelled enough to weep

On The Sixth Of April

Numb
Dead
Empty

A flatline avoided
Only
Because my heart is still beating

I don't want to live
I don't even want to want to live
But my heart beats stubbornly on

The advice is remember
Your reasons to live
Your reasons to stay alive
Your reasons to stay

I'm told I am worth it
I'm told a future of hope awaits me
A way through, a better life,
The shining sun above the fog

But I don't want that
I just want to go home
This longing stronger

Than any reasons to stay

And so
Like an introvert at any party
I must switch instead
To simply choosing
Not to leave

Still

And here I stand
Once again
Heart aching
Mind swirling
Soul wobbling
Body tensing
In readiness to fight or flee the onslaught

Stillness
Is not on the cards
For stillness
Gives time for the weight to crush me
So I must keep moving
Lest it overtake
And I come crashing down

But yet
It has not won
This creeping thief
Tired and longing to stop
I have not fled the fight
I am here
Still

SOS

Headcolds always start the same way for me
A sore scratchy throat
Then stuffy nose and headache
Finally a cough that lingers
Days after all else has disappeared

Some people know when rain is coming
As barometric pressure shifts
Their knees and fingers
Stiffen with anticipation
In air thick and heavy

The shadow is descending once more
Like a weight on my back
Ebbing power like a blackout
After surges of dreams
Alerts to coming danger

The warning signs are there
A chance to batten down the hatches
At the first cough
Before the dreaded storm hits
While there's still light

Throat burns
Pressure shifts
Shadow descends

Here it comes

Batten down the hatches
Send the SOS
Before it's too late

Subtract

I want
to float
away
to disappear
quietly
to take myself
away
without the consequences looming

I'm tired
of looking
into faces
of concern
having nothing
to offer
in return
but blank and empty numbness

I'm ashamed
of voicing
the thoughts
and fears
consuming
swallowing
devouring

whatever or whoever I am

Ouch
I have lost myself
Again
Lost myself
And I am nowhere to be found
Yes
I think that I might
Break
Lost myself again and I feel unsafe

I'm scared
that I
am lost
a stranger
stranded
alone
on streets
dangerous and foreign and cold

The Great Translator

It's taking its toll
I see it on faces everywhere
Furtive and worried
Waiting to be caught out
Or else desperate to escape
For just one moment
The brutal, numbing tightness
Wrapping itself around the days

But there is no escape from this pandemic
Nowhere devoid of its clutches
You can't outrun this ever present threat
Like a storm
Threatening to move in for the kill
Never knowing
When
Or how
It will strike
Never knowing
When
Or if
It will end

But I understand only too well
This global state
Of anger
Fear
Despair
The utter exhaustion
Of living on high alert
Giving way to dejected dullness

Suddenly the beast that haunts my days
Can be translated
The fight to stay afloat
Is in a language everyone can understand
An illness can only be controlled so far
While we do all we can
Sometimes
It pounces
And
It's
Not
Our
Fault

The Note

This week has been rough.
Yesterday was awful.
Today...?
The heaviness is weighing more as the days go by

There is a roster of people
The weekend dotted
With check-ins
The alternative to psych ward detainment

There is another option
But no-one wants me to take it
They all care too much about me
Which just makes it even harder

Yesterday I tried to think
What I would write
In a goodbye note
But I couldn't get past the phrase "I'm sorry"

What do you say
When you just...can't.
When you've had enough.

When the pain is so bad you cant see the next minute.

What picture could I post here
What image shows the eddy
Behind these words
The hamster wheel of hell that I'm not allowed to leave

A black square is too political
A question mark is existential
A grey cloud the artsy kind of melancholy

Or a sheet of paper with just two words...

"I'm sorry".

The Tangled Web

When I was a kid
I used to look for hidey holes
Cubbies and forts
And the spaces under weeping willow branches

I'd make a nest
With all my favourite things
Books and pencils
And a few hours worth of snacks

This end goal in mind
I'd happily explore
Unknown places
Until I found the perfect spot

I say all this
Because I want you to understand
The pull this kind of place has on me

They say the mind
Has over 100 trillion connections
A network of thoughts, instructions, memories

Layers upon layers
The depth of which

Many are reticent to explore

But I am not unfamiliar
With this tangled web
And the lure of these dark, cool, hidden places

Except now my nesting supplies
Consist of -
Well let's just say it's empty and lonely in there

I wish I could write a resolution
A hopeful ending
To this mess of thoughts
But I'm still waiting

This Present Darkness

I know how it feels to have
No hope
No happiness
No light

To feel trapped inside
Your own brain
Your own thoughts
Your own sadness

The sun is shining but I can't see it
It cannot reach me
A darkness so deep no light can penetrate

I know how it feels
To want to stop feeling
To want it to end
To forget what light looks like

Arms of God carry me
Heart of God fight for me
Until I can stand again

Up (It Feels Like Years)

It's been a long cold lonely winter:
Yes it has
The light elusive

The smiles returning to the face:
I'm amazed it remembers how
Muscle memory I guess

I feel that ice is slowly melting:
The rock hard numbness
Softening like butter

It seems like years since it's been clear:
Enough to see above the clouds
Here it comes, the sun